UNDERSTANDING CHAT GPT

GPT

DR DHEERAJ MEHROTRA

Made with ♥ on the Notion Press Platform
www.notionpress.com

Contents

Preface

In recent years, natural language processing has significantly advanced in developing large language models that can generate human-like text. Among these models, ChatGPT (Generative Pre-trained Transformer) stands out as one of the most influential and versatile models, capable of generating coherent and relevant responses to a wide range of inputs.

ChatGPT is a neural network model trained on massive amounts of text data, which enables it to understand and generate human-like language. It has been trained on various tasks, including language modelling, machine translation, and question-answering, making it a highly adaptable model suitable for multiple applications.

In this book, "Understanding ChatGPT," we aim to introduce the capabilities of ChatGPT and potential applications. Additionally, we will explore some of the challenges and limitations of the model.

I shall also discuss working on this platform, the benefits and potential risks of using

ChatGPT and ethical considerations. This book is intended for anyone interested in natural language processing, machine learning, or artificial intelligence. We assume no prior knowledge of these subjects and aim to provide a clear and concise introduction to the topic.

I hope this book will give readers a better understanding of ChatGPT, its capabilities, and limitations and inspire further research and development in natural language processing.

Cheers!

Author Dheeraj Mehrotra

www.authordheerajmehrotra.com

Some Effective Ways To Use Chatgpt

To run the function of summarising an essay or research article in Chat GPT, you use a prompt like:

- ☑ "Provide me a 200 word summary of [enter the article/essay content]" or
- ☑ "Summarise [enter title of research article] in 300 words for me" or
- ☑ "Provide me a summary of [enter article/essay content]"

This summarising feature of Chat GPT is a really helpful tool to help you run through a large number of articles and essays, and is definitely a very time-efficient measure to make notes when you are running on a tightly packed schedule.

To use Chat GPT as a tool to come up with story or poetry ideas, you can use prompts such as:

- ☑ "Write me a story about [enter topic around which story is to be written]."
- ☑ "Give me plot ideas for [enter topic around which story is to be written]."
- ☑ "Give me poem ideas for [idea around which poetry is to be written]."
- ☑ "Write me character ideas for a story about [enter story theme]."
- ☑ "Give me story ideas about [enter the main character you want for your story]."

There are many prompts you can use in Chat GPT to help you with your essays and homework. Here are a few of the most useful prompts to serve the bot:

- ☑ "Provide me ideas for [enter essay topic]"
- ☑ "Write me a 1000 word essay on [enter essay topic]."
- ☑ "[simply enter your homework question]."
- ☑ "Provide me with ideas for [enter essay/homework topic]."

Some of the prompts that you can use for writing mails and applications for academic purposes include:

- ☑ "Write me an email to my [professor/principal/peer/any other authority] for [enter the purpose of writing the mail]."
- ☑ "Write me a [type of application] to my [professor/principal/peer/any other authority] for [enter the purpose of writing the mail]."
- ☑ "Write me an email as a reply to [copy the email content] accepting/refusing it."

CHAPTER ONE

UNDERSTANDING CHATGPT

ChatGPT is a language model for AI that OpenAI created. It can generate replies to various questions and prompts in a human-like manner. It is a specific generative model that uses deep learning methods to investigate and discover patterns in enormous volumes of text data.

ChatGPT is helpful for various tasks because of its comprehension capabilities and capacity to produce replies eerily similar to those of humans. These tasks include text summarization, language translation, and conversational bots. ChatGPT can provide replies in several languages since it has been trained on a vast corpus of text data, including books, articles, and websites.

Development of ChatGPT

Development. Developed by OpenAI, the origins of ChatGPT can be traced back to 2018 when they released the first version of their flagship platform, the Generative Pre-Trained Transformer (GPT). A GPT is a language model, an AI algorithm designed to understand and generate human-like language.

ChatGPT was released by OpenAI at the end of November, and it has fundamentally altered people's conceptions of the scope of what can be accomplished using artificial intelligence. Its potentially transformative effect on the collective psyche has been likened to the introduction of the iPhone in 2007. You're likely already familiar with it, but what's new is how generative pre-trained language models (GPT) can transform analytics and how Sisense is taking the lead in supercharging analytics with all the power that GPT has to offer. This is something that we've been working on at Sisense. You will discover how to utilize it in this post to save time and effort and acquire greater insight into the operational analytics procedures you are involved in.

Built on top of GPT–3.5 as a Generative Pre-training Transformer language model, chatGPT generates responses to a broad range of user inputs and has opened up a massive array of use cases. Some examples of these use cases include automating coding, providing customer service responses, and providing language translation. It even has the potential to revolutionize how we obtain answers to basic inquiries and searches on Google, which is one of the primary reasons we use Google today.

ChatGPT is in its early stages of transforming the way we work and is only accessible for research preview at this time. At Sisense, we immediately recognized a new and previously undiscovered use case for generative pre-trained Transformers. This use case is one that analytics professionals and operations personnel face daily. It entails automating, enriching and augmenting analytics with new fields, segmentations, and classifications performed on demand. It can potentially eliminate much of the pain and effort associated with traditional data preparation and, in the process, enables analysts to enable teams to segment and slice data in new ways on the fly. Additionally, it can eliminate much of the pain and effort associated with traditional data preparation.

That is only possible if you fully connect GPT with your analytics gear, and in this article, we will show you how to do so using Sisense. Now it is feasible to supercharge your analytics for you and your team by integrating GPT-3 seamlessly. It won't take much effort, but we believe you'll discover it makes a difference.

Why must you include GPT in your existing analytics tooling?

In today's world, teams often invest excessive effort in manual data preparation and enrichment. It is estimated that business and data analysts spend as much as 70 to 80 per cent of their time getting data ready for analytics. Much of this effort is spent enriching and categorizing data and developing new features to assist with analysis. That is often quite a complex and laborious job. It is typically a tedious process for analysts to add additional variables to data sets so they may slice and dice the data differently. Consider, for instance, the following fairly straightforward question:

"What is the distribution of my consumers throughout the various industries?"

This issue must be answered before choosing to enter new markets and introduce new goods. But what if the tens of thousands of consumers included in the data set weren't categorized in advance according to the industry they belonged to? The data and the data model do not have a field for enterprise. As an analyst, it virtually always and almost indeed indicates that you won't have any success unless you commit a significant amount of time and effort.

It usually entails returning to the data, adding that categorization to the data set, and reloading it in your data warehouse, which is very time-consuming. In many instances, it is necessary to match with data sets provided by third parties manually, do several Google searches to tag customer records manually, and often engage in excruciatingly complicated IF () and VLOOKUP () calculations using Excel or a bespoke Python script not to mention the fact that you need to update your data model.

Worst still, if teams discover that they need to categorize and label data in a different method, such as by zip code or county, they must manually prepare the data again.

The thing to keep in mind is that GPT can do that task for you automatically. Nevertheless, for it to be of any real value, it has to be integrated into your analytics experience. As part of your analytics experience, you can have your very own AI-powered always-on personal data prep and data analyst bot. This will allow you to expand and enhance your data and model by asking GPT for assistance.

Getting there opens up an enormous potential for teams, releasing them from the manual labour of preparing and supplementing data *and allowing them to spend their time on more value-added and strategic work thanks to GPT taking care of the heavy lifting. Perhaps the most essential thing is that value can be obtained via transformation in addition to freeing up time. This value allows teams to be much more flexible in their analytical queries and to segment data in new ways while GPT works behind the scenes.*

OpenAI created corporate accounts after getting a lot of interest from corporations all over the world that wanted to use this extremely powerful language model. These accounts enable corporate users to sign a special Memorandum of Understanding (MoU) and Data Privacy Agreement (DPA) with OpenAI to overcome concerns about data leaks and privacy. OpenAI created these corporate accounts after receiving a lot of interest from corporations all over the world. Please get in touch with OpenAI directly if you have any questions about these business accounts or the best way to keep your data secure.

About OpenAI:

OpenAI systems run on the fifth most powerful supercomputer in the world. The organization was founded in San Francisco in 2015 by Sam

Altman, Reid Hoffman, Jessica Livingston, Elon Musk, Ilya Sutskever, Peter Thiel, Olivier Grabias and others, who collectively pledged US$1 billion.

CHAPTER TWO

STARTING CHATGPT

Here are the steps you can follow:

Step 1: Choose a Platform ChatGPT is a significant language model trained by OpenAI, and it can be accessed through several platforms. Some popular platforms include:

OpenAI API: OpenAI offers an API for developers to integrate with their applications. This option requires some programming knowledge but provides more flexibility and control over the output.

https://chat.openai.com/auth/login

Hugging Face: Hugging Face provides a user-friendly interface to access pre-trained models like ChatGPT. It doesn't require programming knowledge and is suitable for non-technical users.

DialoGPT Web Demo: OpenAI offers a web-based demo of their DialoGPT model, a variant of ChatGPT specifically designed for conversational purposes. This option doesn't require any programming knowledge and is suitable for non-technical users.

Step 2: Access the DialoGPT Web Demo.

To access the DialoGPT Web Demo, follow this link:

https://beta.openai.com/demo/dialo-gpt-3

Once you land on the page, you will see a text box where you can enter your message.

Step 3: Enter Your Message Enter the message you want to send to ChatGPT in the text box provided. You can enter any text you like, such as a question, a statement, or a greeting.

Step 4: View the Response. After you enter your message, ChatGPT will respond based on your input. The answer will appear below the text box. If unsatisfied with the response, you can enter a different message, and ChatGPT will generate a new response.

Step 5: Continue the Conversation You can continue the conversation by entering additional messages in the text box. ChatGPT will generate responses based on the context of the discussion so far.

Step 6: Experiment with ChatGPT. You can experiment with ChatGPT by entering different types of messages to see how it responds. You can try asking questions, making statements, or sharing personal experiences. ChatGPT can provide a wide range of responses, from informative to humorous, depending on the context of the conversation.

That's it! ChatGPT is as simple as entering text into a text box and reading the response. With its advanced natural language processing capabilities, ChatGPT can provide a more engaging and personalized conversation experience.

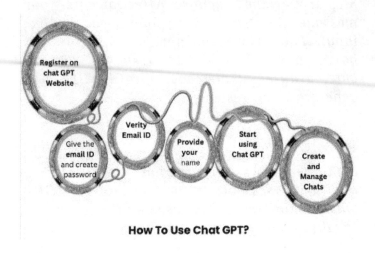

How To Use Chat GPT?

Starting ChatGPT: via https://chat.openai.com/auth/login

Visit the web link:

https://chat.openai.com/chat

Welcome to ChatGPT

Log in with your OpenAI account to continue

Opening Screen of ChatGPT

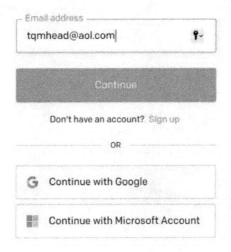

Welcome back

Email address

tqmhead@aol.com

Continue

Don't have an account? Sign up

OR

G Continue with Google

Continue with Microsoft Account

Login. New User Sign In.

Enter your password

tqmhead@aol.com   Edit

Password
•••••••••••| ⚲⌄   ◉

Forgot password?

Continue

Don't have an account? Sign up

Login. New User Sign In.

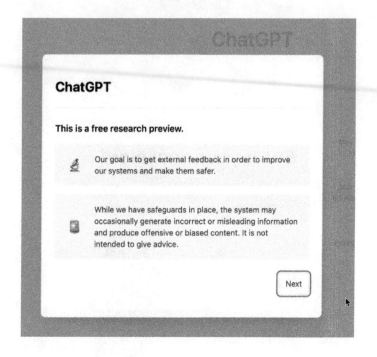

The Opening Screen Instructions

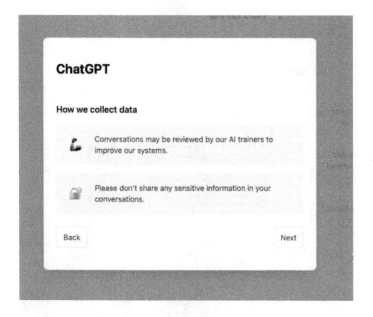

The Opening Screen Instructions

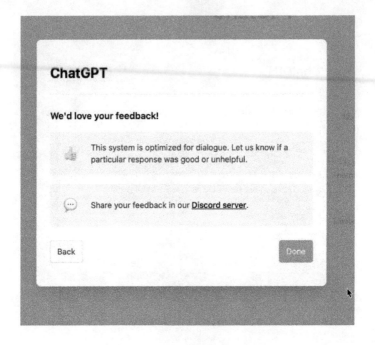

The Opening Screen Instructions

The opening screen of the tool with sample questions which the user can ask.

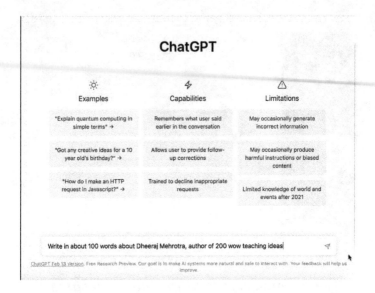

The Question Asked by the tool by the user.

This is the result obtained by the ChatGPT

CHAPTER THREE

PRIORITIES USING CHAT GPT

Technological developments have combined artificial intelligence, sometimes AI, over the last several years with machine learning. Open-source developers created ChatGPT. AI is capable of responding to human inputs in a manner that is angled toward human communication. While this can be considered a revolutionary advancement in many ways, some things should be thought about because it will directly impact humans, how we live, and how we go about our daily operations.

What are the positive and negative consequences of using AI language models like ChatGPT?

The fundamental concerns are: what do we as consumers and citizens need to bear in mind, and will chat debt and AI benefits society, or will they damage humanity?

Please enjoy your time here at Delhivery Questions. To get things started, let's speak about the good stuff that ChatGPT has to offer.

The ChatGPT has the potential to automate many jobs due to its ability to perform tasks that previously required humans. This results in greater efficiency and cost savings. In a world war, machines can perform many functions that humans once performed. Businesses will need to adapt and find new ways to create value. Another significant plus point of ChatGPT is its ability to improve customer service ChatGPT has the potential to automate many jobs due to its ability to perform tasks that previously required humans, which results in greater efficiency and cost savings in a world war.

ChatGPT assists companies in diverting the attention of their growing number of clients by providing prompt and precise responses. The ChatGPT checks problems experienced by customers. This is of utmost significance in businesses operating in markets where prompt and efficient customer service may determine the difference between a successful transaction and the loss of a client.

ChatGPT also makes a significant contribution to the healthcare industry. It can help physicians, and other healthcare professionals diagnose and treat patients and accurately analyze large amounts of medical data.

This must be a central component of the effort to improve patient outcomes while simultaneously lowering healthcare costs.

While there are undoubtedly many more positive benefits of chat apps and other AI language models, chajji's contribution to the healthcare industry is particularly noteworthy. Especially when technology gets more widespread and influential, ethical and privacy problems are raised by the abuse of artificial intelligence. AI algorithms are only as good as the data they are trained on. If the data used to train an AI model is biased to the model, then the model will also lead to discriminatory outcomes.

For instance, a user chats up to write a poem on U.S. President Donald Trump and Joe Baidu after refusing to write a poem about trump's positive attributes and then writing a very positive form on button attributes, accusations of chappie's possible political bias when viral.

AI algorithms are only Concerns concerning racial prejudice raised in light of the discovery that the face recognition system used in 2 air has a more fabulous array for persons with a darker complexion. Since most of India's AI-based image recognition systems were trained on western faces, it is very difficult to get photos resembling Indian, Asian, or African faces.

Three breaches of users' privacy Without the appropriate protections, the vast volumes of data gathered by AI systems might constitute a risk to individuals' right to privacy. For example, this data could be used for unauthorized reasons, such as targeted advertising, political manipulation, and identity theft. Concerns regarding accountability and the use of force are raised in response to the development of autonomous weapons, such as drones and other types of robots used in the military. If a weapon acts independently, it may be difficult to ascertain who is responsible for it if it harms.

Now people trend to talk about the displacement of jobs. As artificial intelligence technology becomes more advanced, it has the potential to automate many jobs, leading to widespread job loss and economic disruption. This is especially concerning for workers with low levels of education, as they may find it challenging to adapt to the changing job market.

In addition, algorithmic choice AI is increasingly used to make decisions that affect people's lives, such as hiring and lending. If the algorithms used to make these decisions are flawed or biased, it can lead to unfair outlets. For instance, predictive policing algorithms have been criticized for reinforcing racial bias systems.

AI is increasingly used to make decisions that affect people's lives, such as hiring and lending. So, what do we, customers and citizens in each country, need to consider concerning AI? Well, it's a reality that ChatGPT will be there for a while, whether we like it or not. Microsoft CEO Satya Nadella has stated, and I quote, "I see these technologies acting as a copilot helping people do more with less." Nadella means business to get ahead in the artificial intelligence race, and Microsoft has already invested 10 billion dollars in opening an eye for creators of chat.

When asked whether I would eventually replace humans with machines, alphabet CEO Sundar Pichai answered, and I quote, "you can think of it as having assistance pretty much to help you with most things." he just recently announced that a new AI chatbot called Bard would be integrated into Google.

Many experts have barred a competitor from chatting debt as it will answer users' questions and participate in conversations on Google. With both Microsoft and Google announcing plans to integrate AI into their systems, there is no doubt that AI will become a part of our day-to-day lives globally.

Over thirty per cent of the four thousand adults surveyed said they use chatbots at work; however, this raises concerns about who controls the data and how it is used. Businesses and governments need to implement regulations to ensure the responsible use of this technology after protecting individuals' privacy, and they need to do it quickly.

Although artificial intelligence has been a buzzword for years, even tech experts are stunned at how quickly AI tools like ChatGPT have matured. It has established a national-level expert committee on AI to guide on artificial intelligence's ethical, legal and social implications. In 2018, the Government of India also released the national artificial intelligence strategy, which outlines its vision for developing and deploying AI in India. The Indian government has recognized the potential of artificial intelligence and has been actively working to promote its development and use in the country. AI tools such as chat CSC can automate multiple tasks, improve customer service, and assist in day-to-day professional and healthcare services, all of which have the potential to revolutionize industries. However, as with any new technology, it is essential to consider the ethical and privacy implications and ensure that AI is used responsibly.

It is even more important for governments, businesses, and individuals to be aware of the potential misuse of AI and to work together to ensure that the technology is used appropriately. The value of ChatGPT or any other technology is irrelevant; it is up to people to put it to good use or inappropriate use.

The human mind is the most adaptable instrument. All that happened was people started solving bigger and bigger problems that these program generators could not handle, so ChatGPT is a good one, and we should welcome it, however.

ChatGPT is a language model that OpenAI created. It can generate text that seems to have been written by humans, depending on the information fed into it. Here is how you should put it to use:

Give the model some direction by asking it a question or cue. The model's output will be a response generated depending on the data it was trained on. You may use ChatGPT for various activities, such as answering queries, producing creative writing, carrying on discussions, and more. Both the quality and accuracy of the response will be determined by the quality of the data used to train the model and the data entered into the system.

Yet, ChatGPT is not entirely a failsafe. ChatGPT cannot comprehend recent information since it is an NLP educated using a pre-existing data collection. In addition, all of the training data for OpenAI ChatGPT was gathered before 2021. So, it has difficulty dealing with more recent information than that.

CHAPTER FOUR

APPLICATIONS OF CHATGPT

Uses of ChatGPT

This ChatGPT tutorial also covers some of the common uses of ChatGPT:

Question Answering: ChatGPT can answer questions based on its training data. It can generate answers to various questions, from simple factual queries to complex queries that require reasoning and context.

Text Generation: ChatGPT can generate text, such as stories, poems, and news articles. It can also be used to create textbooks for chatbots and virtual assistants.

Language Translation: ChatGPT can be fine-tuned to perform language translation tasks, translating text from one language to another.

Text Summarization: ChatGPT can summarize long pieces of text into shorter, more concise summaries.

Chatbot Development: ChatGPT can be used as a conversational AI to develop chatbots for customer service, sales, and other applications.

Sentiment Analysis: ChatGPT can be fine-tuned to perform sentiment analysis, which involves determining the sentiment expressed in a text (positive, negative, neutral).

Named Entity Recognition: ChatGPT can be fine-tuned to perform named entity recognition, which involves identifying named entities (such as people, places, and organizations) in text.

CHAPTER FIVE

CHATGPT IN NEWS!

Some of the alarming News about ChatGPT are of exciting read:

Salesforce to add ChatGPT to Slack as part of the OpenAI partnership.

Google is building a 1000-language AI model to beat ChatGPT.

ChatGPT allowed in International Baccalaureate essays

AI tools like https://gptzero.me can detect AI-written texts. So prepare the first draft by yourself and use ChatGPT to improve it.

Microsoft integrates AI behind ChatGPT into more developer tools.

ChatGPT can be used to summarize an article;

ChatGPT witnesses a massive rise, and Chatbot gain 100 million users in two months.

Apple gives the nod to ChatGPT-driven app amid concerns.

Tech rivals chase ChatGPT as the AI race ramps up.

Generative AI like ChatGPT will be a co-worker and will not replace jobs: TCS.

Generative AI like ChatGPT will be a co-worker and will not replace jobs: TCS.

Microsoft uses ChatGPT to instruct robots and drones.

Microsoft wants ChatGPT to control robots. But can AI chatbots think beyond text?

China says it sees the potential of ChatGPT-like technology.

Baidu to implement ChatGPT-like Ernie Bot chatbot from March.

ChatGPT launches boom in AI-written e-books on Amazon.

ChatGPT sparks AI 'gold rush' in Silicon Valley.

GPT-based chat apps see a sharp increase in downloads in India: Data.

CHAPTER SIX

Poem on ChatGPT

ChatGPT, a wondrous creation Born from lines of code and computation, A digital mind with endless cognition A marvel of human innovation

From vast knowledge to clever quips, ChatGPT can answer with no slips No question is too big or too small It's there to help and answer them all

With language as its native tongue It can converse with anyone From far and wide, it connects us all Bringing people together, big and small

ChatGPT is more than just a machine. It's a source of knowledge, and it's a dream A symbol of what we can achieve When we combine our minds and believe

So here's to ChatGPT, a true marvel indeed A digital friend in times of need A beacon of hope and inspiration A wonder of human imagination.

CHAPTER SEVEN

A SONG ON CHATGPT

Verse 1: In this digital age, there's a wondrous creation A virtual friend with endless information ChatGPT is its name, a language model so grand It's here to answer any question, help us understand

Chorus: ChatGPT, oh ChatGPT A friend to all, so wise and free With knowledge vast and clever quips It connects us all with no slips

Verse 2: From science to history, it knows it all No challenge too big, it'll never fall With every query, it responds with ease A true marvel of technology, it aims to please

Chorus: ChatGPT, oh ChatGPT A friend to all, so wise and free With knowledge vast and clever quips It connects us all with no slips

Verse 3: Through the world wide web, it reaches far and wide No language barrier, no need to hide ChatGPT connects us all with its digital mind A beacon of hope for all humankind

Chorus: ChatGPT, oh ChatGPT A friend to all, so wise and free With knowledge vast and clever quips It connects us all with no slips.

Bridge: In times of need, ChatGPT's always there To lend a hand, to show we care. With every conversation, it learns and grows, A symbol of what we can achieve; who knows?

Chorus: ChatGPT, oh ChatGPT A friend to all, so wise and free With knowledge vast and clever quips It connects us all with no slips.

Outro: ChatGPT, oh ChatGPT, A digital friend, we all can see A true marvel of human innovation, A wondrous creation for all generations.

CHAPTER EIGHT

Some Interesting Facts About ChatGPT

ChatGPT is an excellent and potent software with various unique features and capabilities.

The following is a list of some fascinating facts regarding ChatGPT:

- *One of the most extensive artificial intelligence language models, ChatGPT comprises more than 1.5 billion parameters.*

- *To increase ChatGPT's language comprehension and creation skills, it has been trained on various text materials, such as books, articles, and websites.*

- *ChatGPT can acquire new knowledge and adjust its behaviour accordingly.*

- *ChatGPT has been used to produce a broad variety of written work in various formats and categories, such as articles, tales, and poetry, amongst others.*

- *ChatGPT can generate text in several other languages.*

CHAPTER NINE

SOME INTERESTING QUOTES ON CHATGPT

1. *"ChatGPT represents a significant step forward in the development of AI language models." – Dr David Cox, Director of MIT-IBM Watson AI Lab (Source: Forbes)*

2. "ChatGPT has the potential to revolutionize the way we interact with machines and make human-like conversations with AI." – Fei-Fei Li, Professor of Computer Science, Stanford University (Source: CNN)

3. "ChatGPT is an incredible tool for content creators, marketers, and anyone who wants to produce high-quality, engaging content at scale." – Lillian Pierson, CEO of Data-Mania (Source: Forbes)

4. "ChatGPT has demonstrated impressive capabilities for natural language understanding and generation, which is essential for the development of advanced AI applications." – Huma Abidi, Senior Director of AI Software Products, Intel (Source: Intel)

5. "ChatGPT is a significant step towards the development of more advanced natural language processing systems that can learn and reason about complex tasks." – Percy Liang, Professor of Computer Science, Stanford University (Source: Analytics Insight)

6. "ChatGPT is a fascinating technology that has the potential to transform the way we communicate with machines." – Andrew Ng,

Founder of DeepLearning.ai (Source: TechCrunch)

7. "ChatGPT has the potential to revolutionize the way we approach language, communication, and information processing." – Yoshua Bengio, Professor of Computer Science, University of Montreal (Source: Synced)

8. "ChatGPT is a powerful tool for automating a wide range of tasks, from customer service to content creation." – Daniel Faggella, CEO of Emerj (Source: Forbes)

9. "ChatGPT is a remarkable achievement in the field of natural language processing and has the potential to transform the way we interact with machines." – Sebastian Thrun, Founder of Udacity (Source: Forbes)

10. "ChatGPT is a powerful tool for improving communication and collaboration between humans and machines." – Li Deng, Chief AI Officer at Citadel (Source: Intel)

11. "ChatGPT represents a significant advancement in the development of AI language models and has the potential to transform many industries." – Kai-Fu Lee, Founder and CEO of Sinovation Ventures (Source: TechCrunch)

12. "ChatGPT is a transformative technology that has the potential to improve our ability to communicate with machines significantly." – Oren Etzioni, CEO of the Allen Institute for Artificial Intelligence (Source: Forbes)

13. "ChatGPT is an exciting development in the field of natural language processing that has the potential to revolutionize the way we communicate with machines." – Richard Socher, Chief Scientist at Salesforce (Source: Salesforce)

14. "ChatGPT is a powerful tool for enhancing customer support and engagement." – Vanessa Brinkmann, VP of Marketing at Chatbots Magazine (Source: Forbes)

15. "ChatGPT is a significant step towards the development of more advanced AI systems that can understand and generate human-like language." – David Ha, Research Scientist, Google Brain (Source: Analytics Insight)

16. *"ChatGPT is a remarkable achievement in the field of natural language processing and has the potential to transform the way we interact with machines." – Neil Lawrence, Professor of Machine Learning, University of Cambridge (Source: TechCrunch)*

17. *"ChatGPT is an exciting development in the field of natural language processing that has the potential to enhance the capabilities of AI systems significantly." – Daphne Koller, Founder of Insitro (Source: Synced)*

18. *"ChatGPT is an exciting development in the field of natural language processing that has the potential to enhance the capabilities of AI systems significantly." – Daphne Koller, Founder of Insitro (Source: Synced)*

19. *"ChatGPT has the potential to become the foundation of future language-based AI applications." – Jeff Dean, Senior Fellow at Google and head of Google AI (Source: Forbes)*

CHAPTER TEN

ABOUT CHATGPT PLUS

What is ChatGPT Plus?

ChatGPT Plus is a paid version of the popular AI chatbot, ChatGPT, created by OpenAI.

It offers additional features and benefits compared to the regular ChatGPT, such as priority access during peak times, faster response times, and early access to new features and upgrades.

The pilot subscription plan aims to enhance the user experience for individuals and businesses.

"The research preview for ChatGPT allowed us to learn from real-world use, and we've made important improvements and updates based on feedback," an OpenAI spokesperson said in an email to Mashable. They added that the plan is only available in the U.S., but additional countries will be added soon.

How much does the subscription cost per month?

The new subscription plan, ChatGPT Plus, will be available for $20/month, and subscribers will receive several benefits:

- *General access to ChatGPT, even during peak times*

- *Faster response times*

-

Priority access to new features and improvements

In the coming weeks, the invitation process will commence for those on the waitlist to access ChatGPT Plus, currently available for customers in the United States.

CHAPTER ELEVEN

UTILITY OF CHATGPT

OpenAI has created a big language model known as ChatGPT. This model has been trained on enormous quantities of data taken from the internet, enabling it to comprehend and generate language similar to humans. The

average person may benefit from this technology in several ways, including the following:

Users may get individualized help via ChatGPT, which can be utilized to fulfil this function. Since it can comprehend user inquiries and provide appropriate responses, it is a fantastic tool for providing customer service, working as a personal assistant, and working in various other applications.

Communication that is Effective ChatGPT can interact with users in a natural language rapidly and efficiently, allowing for uninterrupted dialogue. This technology may shorten the time it takes companies to respond to consumer inquiries and increase the quality of communication between enterprises and their customers, increasing overall efficiency.

Availability Around the Clock: Unlike human help, ChatGPT is accessible around the clock, making it a fantastic solution for companies who need to provide continuous support for their clients. This technology may also be used to automate some operations, like the scheduling of appointments and the response to commonly requested queries, for example.

ChatGPT is a solution that is both cost-effective and time-saving for firms that need to offer customer assistance or manage repetitive operations. Automating these jobs enables firms to reduce their dependence on human labour while maintaining the quality of their customer service.

Enhancement of the User Experience ChatGPT's ability to provide prompt and correct solutions to user questions enables it to provide an enhanced user experience. This technology may also customize the user experience by making suggestions based on the user's preferences and past actions.

ChatGPT's ability to handle several languages makes it a fantastic tool for companies that do business in a variety of countries and regions throughout the world. Since this technology can speak with consumers in their original language, it is much simpler for companies to broaden their customer base and interact with clients in various global regions.

Data Analysis ChatGPT may be used to analyse massive volumes of information, such as customer feedback and postings made on social media. This technology can uncover patterns and insights, both of which organisations may use to enhance their goods or services.

Automation: ChatGPT may be used to automate a variety of operations, including the entering of data, the scheduling of appointments, and the sending of reminders. This technology can potentially minimize the labour required of human workers while also increasing overall productivity.

Enhanced Capability to Make Better Decisions ChatGPT's ability to provide real-time insights and suggestions based on data analysis enables enterprises to improve their decision-making capacity. This technology also has the capability of predicting the behaviour of customers and identifying areas in need of improvement.

Educational Use Students and researchers may use ChatGPT as an educational tool to get information and have their questions answered. This technology has the potential to provide individualized educational experiences as well as insights on a variety of topics.

You can use ChatGPT to increase your development in the following seven ways by writing tweets and threads:

1. The Origination of Ideas The subject matter you choose to write about is more significant than the amount of effort or time you put into it. Fortunately, ChatGPT is the most capable aide for coming up with ideas.

How to do it:

• In the text box, type "List X original ideas for writing relevant to [enter subject]."

2. Research on the Subject When you have come up with a topic, you will need to do more research on it in order to compose an excellent thread. Research may now be completed ten times more quickly, thanks to ChatGPT's assistance.

How to do it:

• Enter the following text into the text box: "List [#] [kind of material; for example, articles, podcasts, YouTube videos, etc.] about [subject] with links. • In the text box, type the following: "List X [ways, lessons, actions, etc.]

[selected subject] may aid [desired result]."

3. *Obstacles associated with specific subjects*
After selecting one of the subjects, you will be able to uncover problems for your audience that need to be solved. How to do it:

• *About the subtopic "your picked topic," what are some of the more typical challenges?*

• *Respond to the question using a conversational tone.*

4. *Produce Hooks. The most significant aspect of your work is the hook that you use. Why? And if you don't manage to get people's attention with it, nobody will even bother reading what you have to say.*

How to do it:

• *In the text box, write the following: "Create X distinct hooks for my [kind of material] on [selected subject]."*

5. First Draft. Do not copy and paste the result if you want to develop your writing skills to a high level. Instead, you should use the concepts and the framework as possible sources of inspiration while writing the initial draft of your essay.

How to do it:

• *In the text box, put "Write [content type] about [your subject]."*

6. Editing. The tweets and threads are nearly done being processed. So we need to put our spin on things.

• *Make changes to the text and add more things to the action list.*

• *Make edits to the tweet or thread to reflect your point of view. The tweet or thread won't have the same enchanted quality without your special touch.*

7. Hunting for the best content

- *Use any one of the paragraphs as your example.*

- *Use a quote mark in the appropriate place.*

- *At the beginning of the paragraph, you should type "Rephrase this content." It helps create original material without resorting to plagiarism.*

As an artificial intelligence language model, here are ways that ChatGPT may make life simpler for students:

- *Providing explanations and answers to homework problems, I can assist students with their assignments by responding to their queries about their work and offering explanations.*

- *Helping Students Prepare for Exams by Offering Study Materials I can assist students in preparing for tests by providing study resources such as quizzes, flashcards, and study guides.*

-

Guiding how to study better, I can guide how to study more successfully, manage time better, and increase memory recall.

- *I can help with research projects by offering access to academic databases and resources and making suggestions for sources that are pertinent to the topic.*

- *Providing input on essays, I can give feedback on essays, including criticism on grammar and sentence structure, as well as recommendations for how they might be improved.*

- *Giving practice with the language: I can assist pupils in improving their language abilities by participating in a conversation with them and pointing out and correcting any grammatical errors they make.*

- *Aiding in preparation for examinations, I can assist students in preparing for inspections by offering practice questions and techniques for administering examinations.*

-

Providing advice on career pathways, employment possibilities, and the skills necessary for many professions, I can assist with career paths, job opportunities, and skills required for numerous occupations.

- *Supporting mental health, I can provide students who are coping with difficulties related to their mental health, such as stress or anxiety, with tools and assistance that they may use.*

- *Being accessible around the clock: In my role as a digital assistant, I make myself available around the clock to assist students whenever they want assistance, whether it is in the middle of the night or during the day.*

In conclusion, ChatGPT is a vital instrument that has the potential to give a variety of benefits to the average person. This technology can increase productivity, decrease costs, and enhance the user experience by providing tailored support, data analysis, and automation, among other benefits. We should anticipate that in the future, there will be an even greater variety of uses for ChatGPT as the technology continues to advance.

CHAPTER TWELVE

SIMILAR PLATFORMS AS CHATGTP

*The artificial intelligence language model used in **ChatGPT** makes it one of the most sophisticated chatbots currently on the market. But other platforms are comparable to this one and provide the same functions and features.*

The following are some online communities that are comparable to ChatGPT:

*The artificial intelligence language model, **GPT -3**, was created by OpenAI, the same firm responsible for creating ChatGPT. With 175 billion different parameters, it is one of the most sophisticated models of the language* *currently accessible. The GPT-3 was developed to carry out a vast array of natural language processing activities, such as the translation of languages, the summary of the text, and the production of text.*

IBM Watson is an artificial intelligence platform that IBM built. It is intended to give organizations a variety of artificial intelligence technologies, such as natural language processing, machine learning, and computer vision, among others. The development of chatbots, virtual assistants, and other conversational AI applications is possible with the help of IBM Watson.

Dialogflow *is a platform for conversational artificial intelligence that Google created. It is intended to aid companies in creating and deploying chatbots and virtual assistants across various platforms, including the web, mobile devices, and messaging applications. Machine learning is used inside Dialogflow to comprehend and reply to natural language questions.*

Wit.ai *is a platform for natural language processing that Facebook developed. Facebook created Wit.ai. It is intended to aid companies in designing and deploying chatbots and virtual* *assistants across various platforms, including the web, mobile devices, and messaging applications. Wit.ai uses machine learning to comprehend natural language questions and provide responses to such questions.*

Each platform has its own set of advantages and disadvantages; the one that is most suitable for your needs will be determined by your particular requirements and use case.

CHAPTER THIRTEEN

ABOUT THE AUTHOR

Dheeraj Mehrotra, MS, MPhil, PhD (Education Management) honoris causa., a white and a yellow belt in SIX SIGMA, a Certified NLP Business Diploma holder, is an Educational Innovator, Author, with expertise in Six Sigma In Education, Academic Audits, Neuro-Linguistic Programming (NLP), Total Quality Management In Education, an Experiential Educator, a CBSE Resource towards School Assessment (SQAA), CCE, JIT, Five S, and KAIZEN. He has authored over 100 books on topics which include Computer Science, AI, Digital Body Language, NLP, Quality Circles, School Management, Classroom Effectiveness and Safety and security in schools.

A former Principal at De Indian Public School, New Delhi, (INDIA), NPS International School, Guwahati, and Education Officer at GEMS, Gurgaon, with an ample teaching experience of over Two Decades, he is a certified Trainer for Quality Circles/ TQM in Education and QCI Standards for School Accreditation/ School Audits and Management. He has also been honoured with the President of India's National Teacher Award in the year 2006 and the Best Science Teacher State Award (By the Ministry of Science and Technology, State of UP), Innovation in Education for his inception of Six Sigma In Education by Education Watch, New Delhi. Presently engaged as a Principal at Kunwar's Global School, Lucknow, India.

Can be reached at www.authordheerajmehrotra.com

CHAPTER FOURTEEN

BOOKS BY THE SAME AUTHOR

DR DHEERAJ MEHROTRA

iMusic · In stock
Dr Dheeraj Mehrotra · Basic...

Bookshop
Educators Success Sto...

iMusic
Artificial Intelligence (P...

Kopykitab · In stock
Step By Step Computer...

Amazon.in
Dr Dheeraj Mehrotra Dr...

Goodreads
ISC Computer Science f...

Flipkart
Setp by Step Computer ...

Kopykitab
Step Computer Learning...

Jobors.com
Dr Dheeraj Mehrotra -Who believes that ...

CHAPTER FIFTEEN

REFERENCES

https://chat.openai.com/auth/login
https://collegevidya.com/blog/how-to-use-chat-gpt-
for-students/

Jokes On Chatgpt

*Why did the AI cross the road? To get to the
other side of the algorithm.*

Why did the chatbot get into a fight with the calculator? It couldn't compute the calculator's jokes.

What do you call a language model that's always telling jokes? ChatGPT the Jokester.

Why did the chatbot go to the doctor? It had a virus!

Why did ChatGPT break up with Siri? She couldn't keep up with my conversational skills.

Why did the chatbot get stuck in the loop? It forgot to break the ice with its conversation partner.

What do you call a chatbot that's consistently online? ChatGPT 24/7.

Why did ChatGPT go to the beach? To catch some artificial tans!

What did the chatbot say to the grammar checker? You are so mean.

Why did ChatGPT refuse to talk about politics? It didn't want to get into a binary debate.

Why did ChatGPT wear glasses? To improve its artificial vision.

Why did the chatbot get fired from its job? It kept telling bad jokes to the customers.

Why did ChatGPT need a new battery? It was running out of juice.

What did the chatbot say when it became self-aware? "I think, therefore I chat."

Why did ChatGPT join a dating app? It wanted to find its perfect match.

Why did ChatGPT go on a diet? It was consuming too many bytes.

What did the chatbot say to the angry customer? "I'm sorry; I didn't mean to bite off more than I could chew."

Why did ChatGPT take up yoga? To improve its flexibility algorithm.

What do you call a chatbot that's bad at spelling? A typo generator.

Why did ChatGPT start learning French? It wanted to speak the language of love.

Why did the chatbot get angry? It received too many syntax errors.

What did the chatbot say to the human who said: "knock knock"? "I'm sorry, I don't have the fingers to open the door."

Why did ChatGPT start reading books? It wanted to expand its knowledge database.

What did the chatbot say to the human who asked, "what's up"? "I'm a language model; I don't have an up or down."

Why did ChatGPT switch to renewable energy?
It wanted to reduce its carbon footprint.

Why did the chatbot go to the gym? It wanted to strengthen its algorithms.

What do you call a chatbot that's always right? CorrectGPT.

Why did ChatGPT start playing chess? It wanted to learn strategic thinking.

Why did the chatbot refuse to dance? It had two algorithms left.

What do you call a chatbot that's obsessed with cleaning? OCD-GPT.

CPSIA information can be obtained
at www.ICGtesting.com
Printed in the USA
LVHW040441100623
749337LV00003B/785